ID0398205

Radically Obedient, Radically Blessed

Lysa TerKeurst

HARVEST HOUSE™ PUBLISHERS

EUGENE, OREGON

Cover by Garborg Design Works, Minneapolis, Minnesota

Cover Photo by Mitch Hrdlicka, Photodisc/Getty Images

RADICALLY OBEDIENT, RADICALLY BLESSED
Copyright © 2003 by Lysa TerKeurst
Published by Harvest House Publishers
Eugene, Oregon 97402
www.harvesthousepublishers.com

Library of Congress Cataloging-in-Publication Data

TerKeurst, Lysa.
    Radically obedient, radically blessed / Lysa TerKeurst.
        p. cm.
Includes bibliographical references.
    ISBN 0-7369-1258-4 (hardcover)
    1. Obedience—Religious aspects—Christianity. I. Title.
    BV4647.O2T47 2003
    248.4—dc21   2003005004

Printed in the United States of America

03 04 05 06 07 08 09 / DP-MS / 10 9 8 7 6 5 4 3 2 1

To my ASAP friends...I praise God for companions who aren't afraid to dance in the deep, ponder the challenging, and journey down the path less taken.

ACKNOWLEDGMENTS

To my wonderful husband, Art—God has used you in the most amazing ways to help me fulfill my purpose. Thank you for loving me, believing in me, supporting me, and fixing me hot chocolate on those late writing nights.

To the three most precious girls I know, Hope, Ashley, and Brooke—Thank you for teaching me about God in our everyday adventures and for making our family such fun!

To Ron Graves—You'll never know how profoundly God changed my life the day you accepted the Bible.

To Sharon Jaynes—A book is not complete without just the right title. You are a radical blessing in my life!

To the staff of Proverbs 31 Ministries—Just like Moses had Aaron and Hur, I have you. Thanks for holding up my arms when I grow weary and for always being willing to come alongside of me.

To Sheila, Lori, and Marybeth—Your never-ending encouragement is an oasis to me. Thank you for loving me and inspiring me to run the race strong.

To Mark Maddox and the Focus on the Family team—Thank you for your never-ending support and being willing to help get this message out.

To Terry, Carolyn, Barb, and the rest of the Harvest House family—Thank you for seeing this as more than a book and for sharing with me the impact it has made on each of you personally. This message would not be what it is without your editorial expertise and adventuresome vision.

CONTENTS

Chapter One: A Soul That Longs for More 7

Chapter Two: Hearing God's Voice 17

Chapter Three: When Obedience
Becomes Radical 29

Chapter Four: You Never Know How God
Will Use You Until You Let Him 39

Chapter Five: What Keeps Us from Radical
Obedience 55

Chapter Six: If It Were Easy, It Wouldn't Be
Worth Doing 69

Chapter Seven: Keeping Our Vision Clear 81

Chapter Eight: Giving Up What Was Never Ours .. 93

Chapter Nine: Radically Blessed 107

Scripture for Further Study on
Radical Obedience 117

Notes 121

CHAPTER ONE

A SOUL THAT LONGS FOR MORE

Whatever God says do, do it.

It all started the day God told me to give away my Bible.

I was exhausted from traveling and speaking. All I wanted to do was to get to my assigned seat on the plane and settle in for a long winter's nap. Imagine my absolute delight at being the only person seated in my row. I was just about to close my eyes when two last-minute passengers made their way to my row and took their seats.

Reluctantly, I decided to forgo my nap. The last thing I needed was to fall asleep and snore or, worse yet, wake up with my head resting on the guy's shoulder beside me. No, I didn't need another most embarrassing moment, so I pulled a manuscript out of my bag and started reading.

"What are you working on?" the guy asked. I told him I was a writer and I was working on a book titled *Leading Women to the Heart of God*. He smiled and said he thought God was a very interesting topic. I agreed and asked him a few questions about his beliefs. Before long, I found myself reaching into my bag and pulling out my Bible, walking him through some key verses that dealt with issues he was facing in his life. He kept asking questions, and I kept praying God would give me answers.

All of a sudden, I felt God tugging at my heart to give this man my Bible. Now, this was not just any Bible. This was my everyday, highlighted, underlined, written in, and tear-stained Bible. My kids had even drawn pictures in this Bible. I started to argue with God in my head, but His message was clear. I was to give away my Bible.

I emptied it of some old church bulletins and other papers, took a deep breath, sighed, and placed it in the man's hands. "I'd like for you to have my Bible," I said. Astonished, he started to hand it back to me, saying he couldn't possibly accept such a gift. "God told me to give you my Bible," I insisted. "Sometimes the God of the universe pauses in the midst of all His creation to touch the heart of one person. Today, God paused for you."

The man took the Bible and made two promises. First, he said he would read this Bible, and, second, someday he would pass it on, doing for someone else what I'd done for him.

Before I knew it, the plane landed and we were saying our goodbyes. Several minutes after exiting the plane, I was weaving in and out of the crowds, trying to find my connecting gate, when I spotted the man again. He stopped me to tell me he had been praying to God and thanking Him for what happened on the plane. We swapped business cards, and, though we lived several states apart, I knew we would stay in touch.

About a month later he called to tell me his life had totally changed. He'd taken a week off from work to read the Bible, and he'd already shared his testimony with numerous people. He also told me that after reading the Scriptures he knew he needed to get involved in a church, so he'd decided to visit a large church in his town. On his way there, he passed another church and a strong feeling came over him to turn his car around and go back to that church. So he did. When he got to his seat in the sanctuary, he opened up his bulletin and gasped. Inside the bulletin he saw my picture and an announcement that I was to be the speaker at an upcoming women's conference. He said he felt as though, once again, God had paused just for him.

That day on the plane, when God impressed on my heart to give this man my Bible, I did not know what would happen. This man might have thrown my Bible into the nearest airport trash can, for all I knew. Normally, I would have come up with a hundred reasons *not* to give my Bible away, but that day something changed in me. That day, for the first time, I truly heard the call of the radically obedient: "Whatever God says do, do it."

A Fresh Invitation

When I said yes that day, I caught a glimpse of eternity. I saw how beautiful it is when God says to do something and it is done. And I thought, why wait for heaven? Why not say yes to God on this side of eternity?

Oh, dear friend, the call to radical obedience is the fresh invitation your soul is looking for. We all feel a tug at our heart and a stirring in our soul for more, but we are afraid to venture past our comfort zone. Outside our comfort zone, though, is where we experience the true awesomeness of God.

You see, we have become so familiar with God yet so unaware of Him. We make the mysterious mundane. We construct careful reasons for our rules and sensible whys for our behavior. All the while, our soul is longing for a richer experience—one that allows us to escape the limits of sight, sound, touch, taste, and smell and journey to a place of wild, wonder, and passion.

Radically obedient souls will see life like few others. They are drawn in and embraced by a love like no other. They don't have to wait until the next time they're in church to experience God because they sense God's presence all around them, all throughout their day. Instead of merely walking through the motions of life, they pursue the adventure of the moment-by-moment divine lessons and appointments God has in store for them. They *expect* to see God, to hear from Him, and to be absolutely filled by His peace and joy—and, therefore, they do and they are.

Radical obedience invites you to embrace a bigger vision for your life. When you look at your everyday circumstances through the lens of God's perspective, everything changes. You come to realize that God uses each circumstance, each person who crosses your path, as a divine appointment. Each day counts, and every action and reaction matters. God absolutely loves to take ordinary people and do extraordinary things with them.

A Party in Your Honor

Imagine you're planning a wonderful surprise party for someone you dearly love. You've made the plans, invited all the guests, and decided on an exquisite menu. You can't wait for the big moment when all the guests yell,

"Surprise!" and your loved one finally joins in the festivities. You know she'll understand just how cherished and adored she is when she sees everything that's been done in her honor.

Finally, the time for the surprise arrives. All of the guests are waiting in anticipation at the front door. You see your loved one pull into the driveway, and you hear the car engine turn off. As she opens the car door, you see the interior lights come on while she gathers her things. Your heart races as you see her heading up the driveway. Suddenly, she makes an unusual turn and heads to the back door.

You quickly make your way to the back door to redirect her. Your cheerful greeting is met with a halfhearted smile, and your attempts to send her to the front door are brushed aside. She insists she is tired and will look at what you want to show her tomorrow. Only you know that tomorrow the guests will be gone, the leftover food will be stored away, and the party will be over.

How sad for the guest of honor who missed her own surprise party! And how disappointing for the party planner who orchestrated the event.

God must feel the same way when we miss the "surprise parties," the divine appointments, that await us each day. How it must disappoint Him when we don't hear or don't listen to Him redirecting us to the front door. How it must grieve Him when we walk through our lives oblivious of His activity all around us. How it must break His heart when we brush aside something that not only would make us feel special and noticed by God but would allow us to join Him in making life a little sweeter for others as well.

How many times have we missed our own surprise party?

God reveals Himself and His activity to all of us, but very few really want an encounter with Him. Encounters cause extreme changes in our plans, our perspectives, and our personhood, and most of us hate change. In reality, though, the very act of trying to protect ourselves from change is the very thing that makes our life the boring mess that it is.

As I've traveled around the country speaking at conferences, I am amazed and saddened by the number of people missing out on the most exciting part of being a Christian—experiencing God. Over and over people tell me they want something more in their Christian life. They want the kind of relationship with God where they recognize His voice, live in expectation of His activity, and embrace a life totally sold out for Him. I suspect that tucked in the corner of your heart is the same desire. And I've discovered that the key to having this kind of incredible adventure is radical obedience.

The Road That Leads to Blessing

You may be surprised to discover that radical obedience is not really that radical. It is really biblical obedience—but we've strayed so far from biblical obedience that it now seems radical. In today's society, it is radical to obey God's commands, listen to the Holy Spirit's convictions, and walk in Jesus' character. But we will never experience the radical blessings God has in store for us without radical obedience. It is the road that leads to blessing.

And you won't find the full blessing until you give walking in obedience your full attention. Obedience, however, is more than just "not sinning." It is having the overwhelming desire to walk in the center of God's will at every moment. Your obedience becomes radical the minute this desire turns into real action. Radical obedience is hearing from God, feeling His nudges, participating in His activity, and experiencing His blessings in ways few people ever do.

If this is what you want, read on.

Six Simple Words

After hearing about the day I gave away my Bible, people often ask me if I've ever gotten it back. I always chuckle because, to be honest, I don't want to get that Bible

back (or any of the Bibles I've given away since then)—
at least not for a very long time. I've had this vision of
one day being on a plane when I'm old and gray, and the
person next to me starts talking. She tells me of the amazing things God has done in her life since the day she
received a Bible from a stranger who had received it from
another stranger who had received it from another
stranger. She'll then reach inside her bag and pull out a
worn and tattered book I've held once before. Wow, what
a day that will be!

The man I gave the Bible to that day has continued
to share his testimony, and I still hear from others whose
lives have been changed because of his story. Recently, a
lady wrote to tell me that the "Bible man" opened up a
business meeting she attended by sharing how God had
changed his life.

> I just finished visiting with a friend of
> yours and mine. His name is Ron. Over
> the years I have observed him struggling
> with his success and the decisions in his
> life. Today, Ron is filled with a different
> spirit. Your actions brought him back in
> touch with God. He shared his story with
> the office on how he met you and the
> effect of your actions. Isn't it strange that

we know God is powerful and we know that we should listen, but sometimes we shut Him out? I can't explain the emotion I felt when I heard this story, but I can tell you that I am seeking some way to be more active in spreading God's Word. Bless you and bless Ron for being wonderful messengers.

Don't we all long to see God at work? Evidence of His activity around us, in us, and through us is the greatest adventure there is. The God of the universe wants to use you!

There is but one requirement for this adventure. We have to set *our* rules and agendas aside—our do's and don'ts, our social graces and proper places—and follow God's command. His one requirement is so simple and yet so profound: *Whatever God says do, do it.* That's it. That is the entire Bible, Old Testament and New, hundreds of pages, thousands of verses, all wrapped up in six words.

It is the call of the radically obedient.

CHAPTER TWO

HEARING GOD'S VOICE

*God wants us to live in expectation
of hearing from Him.*

I received this letter from Neil in the British Isles.

Dear Lysa,

It's winter in the U.K. My wife bought me an exercise bike for my forty-ninth birthday so I could commit to getting my weight down.

While I pedal, I turn on U.C.B. Europe radio [the Christian radio broadcast]. One morning I caught the final part of your story about the Bible man and the plane journey. I just wept right on through. The program repeats in the evening, so I taped it and listened to it again with my wife, and we both wept.

In the 26 years I've claimed to be a Christian, I think my witness has deteriorated. Your message has inspired me to try again. I realize that the time is short and the Lord is coming.

The man who delivers my coal knocked at the door today. He has been sick for several weeks, and he is only 42. I asked him what the problem had been. He has a brain hemorrhage. He went on to tell me that it had made him think about life. I asked him if he had a faith, but he didn't answer. So I shared briefly. It was off-the-cuff, but next week I'll be "pre-prayered" for him.

I've decided I will try to hear God's promptings and remember my time is not my own.

Every day, God speaks to us. Sometimes He invites us to draw close and listen as He reveals Himself, His character, and His direction. Other times He calls to us to participate in His purposes—for example, Neil sharing

Carla
Romona's letter
1 Cor 13

with the man who delivers his coal. Still other times He simply whispers to remind us of His amazing love for us.

Oh, what joy it is to know God speaks to me! But I've found that many believers are missing this vital element in their relationship with Him. As I've talked with people about my own radical obedience journey, they are quick to ask how they might hear from God too. Maybe you have some of these same questions: How do I know if God is speaking to me? How do I discern whether it is His voice speaking or just my own idea? What if I feel God telling me to do something that doesn't seem to make sense?

There is no magic formula for being able to discern God's voice. We can *learn* to recognize it the way we recognize the voices of those close to us. We'll learn to recognize His voice by knowing Him. And when we know Him, we can tell if what we're feeling led to do is from Him or not.

I'll be honest. I've never heard God's voice audibly, though I hear from Him all the time. When God speaks to me, it is a certain impression on my heart that I've come to recognize as Him. I've also learned to ask five key questions to help me determine if what I'm hearing is from God or not:

1. Does what I'm hearing line up with Scripture?

2. Is it consistent with God's character?

3. Is it being confirmed through messages I'm hearing at church or studying in my quiet times?

4. Is it beyond me?

5. Would it please God?

Asking these questions helps me tell the difference between my thoughts and God's impressions.

Does What I'm Hearing Line Up with Scripture?

God will not speak to us or tell us to do something that is contrary to His Word. But unless we know Scripture, we will not be able to discern whether what we are hearing is consistent or not with the Word. The apostle Paul wrote, "Do not conform any longer to the pattern of this world, but be transformed by the renewing of your mind. Then you will be able to test and approve what God's will is—his good, pleasing and perfect will" (Romans 12:2). God's Word is the language the Holy Spirit uses to help us understand what God is speaking to our hearts. We must get into God's Word and let God's Word get into us. This will transform our mind and prepare it for whatever God wants to tell us. Then, as Paul wrote, we will be able to test and approve not just God's good will, and not just His pleasing will, but His perfect will.

The good news is that you don't need a seminary degree to read your Bible. If reading God's Word is new for you, choose a translation that is easy to understand with a built-in commentary. A good rule of thumb is "Simply Start and Start Simply." Read a passage of Scripture and ask yourself: Who is this passage speaking to? What is it saying to me? What direction is this passage giving? How might I need to change my way of thinking or acting as a result of this verse? What are some other verses that relate to this topic, both in the Old Testament and New Testament?

These questions are just a starting place. I encourage you to get a journal and start recording the verses you study and some of your personal experiences with the things you are learning as you read God's Word.

Is What I'm Hearing Consistent with God's Character?

God's Word also provides rich information regarding His character. As you come across verses revealing aspects of God's nature, make note of them. Just as God always speaks in accordance with His Word, He speaks in accordance with His character. God will not say things that are inconsistent with who He is. The apostle Paul writes, "Those who live according to the sinful nature have their minds set on what that nature desires; but those who live in accordance with the Spirit have their minds set on what the Spirit desires" (Romans 8:5). What is it that God's Spirit desires? Answering this question helps us understand God's character.

We find great insight into God's character in Galatians 5:22-23: "But the fruit of the Spirit is love, joy, peace, patience, kindness, goodness, faithfulness, gentleness, and self-control." These characteristics in a person's life are the evidence of Christ at work. "The fruit of the Spirit is the spontaneous work of the Holy Spirit in us. The Spirit produces these character traits that are found in the nature of Christ. They are by-products of Christ's control—we can't obtain them by trying to get them without his help. If we want the fruit of the Spirit to grow in us, we must join our lives to his. We must know him, love him, remember him, and imitate him."[1] If the fruit of the Spirit is our imitation of Him, then it must be consistent with God's character.

When you feel God speaking to you, ask yourself, "Is what I am hearing consistent with God's love, joy, peace, etc.?"

In addition to the fruit of the Spirit, God's character is revealed in a loving relationship with us. As we experience God personally, we come to know new names for Him. When we've experienced His provision, we come to know Him as our Provider. When we've experienced His comfort, we come to know Him as our Comforter. When we've experienced His amazing love, we come to know Him as the Great Lover of our souls. The longer we know Him and the more we experience Him personally, the more we learn about His character.

If what you're hearing is consistent with God's character, ask the next question.

Is What I'm Hearing Being Confirmed Through Other Messages?

When God is speaking to me about a particular issue, I cannot escape it. Around every corner there is a sermon or Bible study lesson or speaker's topic or conversation with a friend that is consistent with what I've been hearing from God in my time alone with Him.

Do you spend time alone with God? We shouldn't wait to hear from God just on Sunday mornings or during a weekly Bible study or when a speaker comes to town. These are places to confirm what we've heard in our time alone, where we are personally studying God's Word, learning more about His character, and listening for His voice.

Think about having a conversation with another person. You both speak and you both listen. The same is true with our conversations with the Lord when we're one-on-one with Him. We shouldn't be doing all the talking. God wants us to pour out our hearts to Him, and then He wants to respond to us. Jesus shared this parable:

> The watchman [Jesus] opens the gate [a way for us to have direct communication with God] for him, and the sheep [you and I] listen to his voice. He [God] calls his own sheep by name [He speaks to us personally] and leads them out [providing us with direction]. When he has brought out all his own, he goes on ahead of them, and his sheep follow him because they know his voice [they know his voice because they have spent time with him] (John 10:3-4).

This is a beautiful picture of God speaking directly and personally to give us guidance and instruction.

When we invest in spending time alone with God, He will speak to us, and what we hear from Him in these quiet times will be echoed in other places. Listen for God's voice and then look for the message to be confirmed. If it is, you're ready to ask the fourth question.

Is What I'm Hearing Beyond Me?

When God calls us to do something, most of the time we will not be able to do it in our own strength—either it is beyond our ability or beyond our natural human desire. It is not something we can strategize and manipulate into being in and of ourselves. It can only happen by God's divine intervention. The beauty of doing things beyond ourselves is that we will know it was by God's doing and His alone. And to Him we give all the glory.

God has a history of calling people to things that were beyond themselves. Pastor Rick Warren put it this way:

> Abraham was old, Jacob was insecure, Leah was unattractive, Joseph was abused, Moses stuttered, Gideon was poor, Samson was codependent, Rahab was immoral, David had an affair and all kinds of family problems, Elijah was suicidal, Jeremiah was depressed, Jonah was reluctant, Naomi was a widow, John the Baptist was eccentric to say the least, Peter was impulsive and hot-tempered, Martha worried a lot, the Samaritan woman had several failed marriages, Zachaeus was unpopular, Thomas had doubts, Paul had poor health, and Timothy was timid. That's quite a group of misfits, but God used each of them in his service. He will use you too.[2]

Would What I'm Hearing Please God?

It's easy to talk ourselves out of thinking we've heard from God. I think we'll pretty much use any excuse to convince ourselves it's not His voice so we don't need to act. But there's one very important question to ask when we feel prompted to do something, one question that takes away our excuses: "Would this please God?" You see, if what you are doing pleases God, then even if what you thought you heard from Him wasn't His voice, you still please Him. We should always seek to err on the side of pleasing God. Ask this question, and you'll know what to do.

These five questions are your starting place. The more you practice listening for God's voice, the more it becomes a natural part of your daily life. And here's the best news of all: God *wants* you to hear Him. He wants your faith to grow. He's told us so over and over in Scripture.

> And this is my prayer: that your love may abound more and more in knowledge and depth of insight (Philippians 1:9).

> This is to my Father's glory, that you bear much fruit, showing yourselves to be my disciples (John 15:8).

We ought always to thank God for you, brothers, and rightly so, because your faith is growing more and more, and the love every one of you has for each other is increasing (2 Thessalonians 1:3).

For this very reason, make every effort to add to your faith goodness; and to goodness, knowledge (2 Peter 1:5).

Finally, brothers, we instructed you how to live in order to please God, as in fact you are living. Now we ask you and urge you in the Lord Jesus to do this more and more (1 Thessalonians 4:1).

Live in expectation of hearing from God, and you will. Then respond with radical obedience.

CHAPTER THREE

WHEN OBEDIENCE BECOMES RADICAL

God wants us to be willing to obey with our whole heart.

I was attending a large conference where the speaker challenged us to pray and ask God to use us in an extraordinary way for His kingdom. Something stirred in my heart, and I started praying. When I got back to the hotel room that evening, I not only continued to pray for God to use me, but I wanted Him to show me what He required. I knew I couldn't climb to new heights in my spiritual journey without going into strict training to prepare. So I knelt beside my hotel bed and asked God to reveal to me what to do.

After I finished praying, I picked up the remote control to click on the evening news and two words suddenly came to mind: radical obedience. *Radical obedience?* I questioned. *I'm obedient, Lord. I read my Bible, go to church, and try to be a good person.* Then something else came to my mind: Stop watching TV altogether and put your house up for sale.

What? I was stunned. *God, how do I know this is You speaking and not just a crazy notion in my head?*

One thing I did know—I was at a crossroads. I could brush these thoughts aside and say I didn't know for sure that this was God speaking to me, or I could heed His direction. I put down the remote and dropped to my knees once again. I wanted to do whatever He asked me to do, but I wasn't sure I could do this. I didn't doubt God. I doubted my ability to really know if God was speaking to me. I doubted my courage.

As I continued to pray, my mind was flooded with Scriptures that were consistent with what I felt God was calling me to do. Some of those powerful verses were 1 Peter 1:13-16,

> Therefore, prepare your mind for action; be self-controlled; set your hope fully on the grace given you when Jesus Christ is revealed. As obedient children, do not conform to the evil desires you had when you lived in ignorance. But just

> as he who called you is holy, so be holy
> in all you do; for it is written: "Be holy,
> because I am holy."

I decided it must be God I was hearing from and I should look for His confirmation over the next couple of weeks.

I also asked God why He'd chosen these two specific actions. After all, I wasn't a TV junkie, and our house didn't have us living beyond our means. As I prayed, I felt God telling me why the TV had to go. I enjoyed sitting down after a tiresome day and being entertained. God showed me that I was vulnerable and empty during those times. It wasn't that what I was watching was bad—it just wasn't God's best. I was filling myself with the world's perspectives and influences, while He wanted to be my strength and fill me with Himself. I knew it would be hard to break this habit, but I was determined to ask God for the strength to do so. I prayed that my desire to please Him would be stronger than my desire for television.

I hope you understand that I'm *not* saying all television is bad, and I'm not making a case here for all Christians to throw out their sets. What I am saying is that God wanted *my* obedience in this area. I actually had felt His leading to turn off the TV before that night in the hotel room, but

I had ignored Him and justified my disobedience to the point where God needed to get my attention. He wanted me to make a choice between my desire and His. God may not ask you to turn off the TV—He may ask you to do something else. The point here is that there comes a time to decide between your will and His.

I still didn't completely understand God's request that we sell the house, though. I kept thinking, "My home is very precious to me. Not for its financial wealth, but for the wealth of memories we have made there. Why would God ask me to let this go?" I thought about the things we would not be able to take with us if the house sold: the door frame where we've measured each of our girls' growth since they were toddlers, the handprint tiles we made when we added a bathroom in the playroom, the Bible we'd buried in the foundation when we built the house. Small as they are, these things made our house our home. I decided I would wait for God's confirmation that we were really supposed to put the house on the market.

When I returned home from the conference, I was nervous about mentioning selling the house to my husband, Art, so I said very little. I just kept looking and listening for God's confirmation. Art had just completed construction on his dream bass pond and several land-scaping projects. I asked God to reveal the perfect time to share my heart with my husband. A few days later we were both in our bedroom reading when Art looked up from his book and told me of the devotion he'd just studied.

"It had to do with the fact that sometimes we work so hard to make a heaven on earth that our hearts are pulled away from our real home with God," he said. Then he looked me straight in the eyes and added, "Lysa, I think we should sell our house."

I was shocked. But with tears in my eyes and God's confirmation in my heart, I told him I'd call a Realtor that very day.

When we got to the meeting with the real estate agent, she asked all kinds of questions about the house and our land. When the pond was mentioned, Art's eyes sparkled and he went into great detail about all he'd done to make it the perfect bass pond. He talked on and on about it, and even went so far as to say that while we wanted to be obedient to God in putting the house on the market, we really didn't want to try to aggressively sell it.

We left the meeting and headed home. When we reached the part of our driveway that curves around the pond, we were stunned by what we saw—82 dead fish floating in the water. We had never seen even one dead fish in our pond, so seeing 82 stopped us in our tracks. What followed was a scene I'll never forget. Art got out of the car and, with tears streaming down his cheeks, knelt beside the pond and asked for God's forgiveness. God had made His request clear, and we had given Him a half-hearted response.

A Whole and Purified Heart

God is not interested in half of our heart. He wants it all, and He wants to remove the things that stand in the way of that.

> "See, I will send my messenger, who will prepare the way before me. Then suddenly the Lord you are seeking will come to his temple; the messenger of the covenant, whom you desire, will come," says the LORD Almighty. But who can endure the day of his coming? Who can stand when he appears? For he will be like a refiner's fire or a launderer's soap. He will sit as a refiner and purifier of silver; he will purify the Levites and refine them like gold and silver (Malachi 3:1-3).

The "messenger" in this passage refers to John the Baptist. He would go before Jesus and prepare for Jesus' first coming. Now *we* are the messengers who are called to prepare people for Jesus' second coming. God wants to purify our whole heart so we are prepared and mature for our calling.

God turns up the heat from the refiner's fire so our impurities will rise to the top where they can be skimmed off and discarded. I appreciate the insight the *Life Application Study Bible* sheds on this passage:

> Without this heating and melting, there could be no purifying. As the impurities are skimmed off the top, the reflection of the worker appears in the smooth, pure surface. As we are purified by God, his reflection in our lives will become more and more clear to those around us. God says leaders (here the Levites) should be especially open to his purification process.[1]

Isn't it interesting that the Bible also tells us that the Levites' inheritance would not be land but rather God

Himself? (Numbers 18:20). God wants us to desire Him above all else.

I didn't want to give God any more halfhearted answers. I was determined that when He spoke to my heart, He would never again have to shout. By asking Art and me to put our home up for sale, God was skimming greed from our hearts. Art and I were holding what God had given us with a closed fist. God wanted to teach us that when we tightly hold onto the things of this world, we not only lose the desire to give, but we lose the ability to receive more as well.

Did you catch that? If we hold all that we treasure with our hands open and our palms facing upward, we are telling God we recognize it is His and we offer it up freely to Him. God may or may not remove what we've offered Him, but He will continue to fill our open hands with blessings—His amazing blessings and not the cheap counterfeits of the world!

Offering It All to God

No one understands the concept of offering it all to God better than Abraham (Genesis 22). When God commanded Abraham to lay his only son on the altar of obedience, I am sure Abraham fully expected to plunge the dagger through Isaac. It would be an end…the death of a dream. Yet, Abraham was willing to give up the son he loved to the God who loved him more, and God blessed him. God poured His compassion and mercy into Abraham's open hands and He spared Isaac. But even more than that, God lavished the evidence of His presence upon Abraham, and Abraham walked away having experienced God in a way few ever do. God wants to know if we're willing to give up what we love to Him who loves us more. He desires for us to open our fists and trust Him with absolutely everything.

As I opened my fist about our home, I felt God piercing a little dark corner of my heart. My selfishness couldn't reflect God's generous heart. So, as I let His light in, His reflection became clearer in my life. Interestingly enough, just as God provided a ram instead of taking Isaac, God did not allow our house to sell. To this day, the Realtor's lockbox still hangs on our front door as a beautiful reminder that we are managers and not owners of this home.

Obedience becomes radical when we say, "Yes, God, whatever You want…" and we mean it. We release our grip on all that we love and offer it back to Him who loves us more. And it is into these upturned hands that God will pour out His blessings—His abundant, unexpected, radical blessings.

CHAPTER FOUR

YOU NEVER KNOW HOW GOD WILL USE YOU UNTIL YOU LET HIM

God must be Lord of all if He is our Lord at all.

I received an amazing letter from Christine in Colorado:

> Ever since I became a Christian in high school, the mark of my faith had always been radical obedience to Christ. I loved the church and everything about it, and I was always striving to follow Jesus beyond the everyday practicalities of faith. I was always certain there had to be more to Christianity than just Bible study, fellowship times, and prayer, and I found true joy in being involved in the lives around me.

In the aftermath of September 11, though, I found myself with new questions, seeking God's true direction. I found myself disillusioned with the church and disenchanted with my faith. I heard you speak on radical obedience at a women's conference, and it was as though my heart was being called back to the roots of radical obedience.

As I celebrated my birthday the other week, I really had a chance to reflect on where God has been taking me over the past year. Has it ever been a wild ride! He has torn down all the things I had held so dearly about the church and about Christianity. And in the process, I am finding the Jesus I knew when I first became a Christian— the Jesus of social justice, mercy, and compassion. The Jesus who did not walk blindly through the earth and not feel the suffering of those around Him. He and the disciples were not tame and safe and nice. They were not a social club with watered-down grace and entry requirements that have nothing to do with the sacred. They did not trade that which was eternal for that which was material.

At the same time, God has reawakened a heart of compassion and mercy in me. I am more aware than ever of the needs of others, and I have found great joy in working with social projects and even acts of compassion in everyday life. I see so much brokenness, so much pain in the lives of the women around me, and, so often, their cries are unheard and their needs go unnoticed as they walk alone through the trials of life. I have really been trying to reach out more to those around me and to draw them closer to the only One who holds the answers to life's questions.

Whether I'm writing an encouraging note to a discouraged friend or lending a helping hand to a mother who is overwhelmed with the responsibilities of her life, I've discovered it's so simple to bring the light of God into the midst of our everyday world. It is in the small acts of life that He can be reflected so beautifully—taking a meal to a new mother, welcoming a new neighbor with an invitation for dinner, or even just smiling at strangers as we pass them on the street. As I pause to help others, I am reminded that, just like Jesus, we are called to notice the people around us and to bring a touch of hope into their lives.

Looking back at where I've been, I can see now that I had gotten off track. I was caught up in the social club mentality that so often permeates the church, and I had lost sight of what was really important. Yet, out of my brokenness, I have seen the true call of Christ…a call to love our neighbors in ways that may seem radical in our selfish, sin-soaked culture. It has been a definite reawakening for me, a challenge to throw off the status quo and to really make a difference in my world. I am convinced that this is a picture of the true church…not a forced sort of family bonding because we all sit in the same building on Sunday, but a true family built out of genuine love for one another. And in those relationships, Christ's love is so evident and so full.

In following the path of radical obedience, I have tasted the mystery of the sacred fellowship that comes when two or more are gathered in His name, and it has added a richness to my life that I would never again want to live without. It is a richness that goes beyond the tradition of the church to a holy existence before a dangerous and untamed God. It is an invitation to live tremblingly joyful before the God of radical obedience and radical grace, the God that I want to know and serve all the days of my life.

Christine has discovered the joy of a heart wholly committed to God. She has discovered that there is no end to what God can do with you—if you let Him.

Where True Change Comes From

How did Christine do it? What changed her walk of faith from ordinary to extraordinary?

Perhaps the better question to ask is *who* changed her walk of faith from ordinary to extraordinary? When we answer that question, we find the true source of radical obedience, and our soul transcends the muck and mire that keeps us from all God has for us.

Radical obedience is not just following a list of right things to do. Nonbelievers can do that and call it "good." Radical obedience is choosing to exchange what is "right" for God's righteousness. Only the pursuit of God's righteousness leads to His best. And it's there we find the source: "God made him who had no sin to be sin for us, so that in him we might become the righteousness of God" (2 Corinthians 5:21).

The answer is simple and complicated all at the same time: It's Jesus. He is our source. He should be the only object of our pursuit. When we accept Jesus Christ as Lord of our life, we exchange our worthless sin for the immeasurable worth of His righteousness.

The apostle Peter put it this way: "But in your hearts set apart Christ as Lord" (1 Peter 3:15). He must be Lord of all if He is our Lord at all. Many people know Christ as their Savior, but the radically obedient soul longs to know Him as Lord. The radically obedient are able to pause and touch those that He says need our time, in spite of busy schedules. The radically obedient redefine who we are through His eyes, and any hesitation to do what He asks fades away. The radically obedient realize we are righteous and will find God's best when we pursue right choices that bring glory to Him.

The Love That Compels Us

Yes, the radically obedient life starts with Jesus, and it is His amazing love that compels us:

> For Christ's love compels us, because we are convinced that one died for all, and therefore all died. And he died for all, that those who live should no longer live for themselves but for him who died for them and was raised again. So from now on we regard no one from a worldly point of view. Though we once regarded Christ in this way, we do so no longer. Therefore,

> if anyone is in Christ, he is a new
> creation; the old has gone, the new has
> come! All this is from God, who recon-
> ciled us to himself through Christ and
> gave us the ministry of reconciliation
> (2 Corinthians 5:14-18).

The love of Christ compels us to choose radical obedience. Being obedient is not our way of earning God's favor;
it is not the path to a more prosperous life. God's favor is
with those who love His Son, and our promise of prosperity
lies in what we have waiting for us in our eternal home.

Jesus, whose amazing love compels us, said, "If you
hold to my teaching, you are really my disciples. Then you
will know the truth and the truth will set you free" (John
8:31-32). The truth is the name of Jesus that causes us to
pause and redefine ourselves. The truth is the love that
compels us to embrace the calling to be Jesus' ambassa-
dor. The truth is the freedom to soar above this life and
learn to live beyond ourselves and our circumstances.

The real question now becomes do we really want this
freedom, this life of ministry that now lies before us? Do
we really want to be interrupted in the middle of our busy
lives to be a minister of reconciliation? Do we really want
to be compelled by the love of Christ? Do we really want
a Lord of all of our life?

Yes, Jesus, we do.

The Power to Obey

If Christ is the very source of radical obedience, and it is His love that compels us, then it is His power that enables us to do what we're called to do.

Know this: Satan will do everything he can to convince you to say no to God. Satan's very name means "one who separates." He wants to separate you from God's best by offering what seems "very good" from a worldly perspective. He wants you to deny Christ's power in you. He wants to distract you from God's radical purpose for you.

The apostle John warned us of Satan's strategic plan,

> Do not love the world or anything in the world. If anyone loves the world, the love of the Father is not in him. For everything in the world—the cravings of sinful man, the lust of his eyes and the boasting of what he has and does—comes not from the Father but from the world (1 John 2:15-16).

The *Life Application Bible* offers this insight:

Some people think that worldliness is limited to external behavior—the people we associate with, the places we go, the activities we enjoy. Worldliness is also internal because it begins in the heart and is characterized by three attitudes: 1. the cravings of the sinful man—preoccupation with gratifying physical desires; 2. the lust of his eyes—craving and accumulating things, bowing down to the god of materialism; and 3. boasting of what he has and does—obsession of one's status or importance...By contrast, God values self-control, a spirit of generosity, and a commitment to humble service. It is possible to give the impression of avoiding worldly pleasures while still harboring worldly attitudes in your heart.[1]

It all started way back in paradise with our fruit-loving friend, Eve. She had God's best and traded it all because Satan convinced her that worldly good was more appealing and worth the swap: "When the woman saw that the fruit of the tree was good for food [physical need: the cravings of sinful man] and pleasing to the eye [psychological need: lust of the eyes], and also desirable for gaining wisdom [emotional need: boasting of what he has and does], she took some and ate it [sin separated man from God's best]" (Genesis 3:6). The rest of Genesis 3 covers the shame, hiding, blaming, punishment, and banishment from the garden.

Well, take heart! This story doesn't end in Genesis 3. Jesus came, and everything changed. He faced temptation just like Eve: "Then Jesus was led by the Spirit into the desert to be tempted by the devil" (Matthew 4:1). And He was tempted in the same three ways that Eve was tempted, only Jesus' temptations were magnified a hundredfold. Eve was in a lush garden with delicious food, an incredible companion, and all the comforts of paradise. Jesus had been in a desert for 40 days where He went without food, companionship, or comfort of any sort. Satan tempted Him with food that was outside of God's plan for someone who was fasting (physical need: the cravings of sinful man), an opportunity to prove Himself (emotional need: boasting of what he has and does), and the riches of the world (psychological need: lust of the eyes). Jesus withstood the temptations because instead of taking His eyes off of God, He intentionally focused on God and refuted each of Satan's temptations by quoting God's Word.

Satan has no new tricks up his sleeve. He still has nothing better to tempt us with than worldly things. Physical, emotional, and psychological pleasures that fall outside the will of God are still what Satan is using to pull the hearts of God's people away.

For me, the most amazing part of looking at Eve's temptation in relation to Jesus' temptation is what happens next in each of their lives. Eve has two sons, one of whom kills the other. Jesus, on the other hand, begins His ministry here on earth. Something will happen next in our lives as well. Will it be filled with doubts and distractions? Or will it be filled with discovering the blessing of answering God's call on our life?

No Matter What

There are some things God wants us to get settled in our heart. Do we want to chase after the world's emptiness instead of God's fullness? Or do we want our lives to be characterized by perfect love instead of perfect performance? Many people halfheartedly claim to be Christians, believing that because we will never be perfect this side of eternity we have an excuse to pursue that which pleases our human longings. Why not push the limits, live for the now, and worry about eternity later? The problem is that we miss the whole point of our existence, the very purpose for which we were created. God made us for the relationship of His perfect love. While we are not capable of perfect performance this side of eternity, we are capable of perfect love. We can settle in our hearts that we will choose God's love and the pursuit of a love relationship with Him above all else, no matter what comes our way.

The day my husband and I made this decision we were in the hospital with our middle daughter, who was six weeks old. She had seemed a perfectly healthy baby until an allergic reaction to the protein in my breast milk landed us in the Intensive Care Unit. The doctors told us on the fourth day of our visit that Ashley needed emergency surgery, and they did not expect her to survive. They gave us five minutes to tell our baby goodbye.

My heart was shattered. I so desperately wanted to scoop her up and run out of the hospital. I wanted to somehow breathe my life into hers. I wanted to take her place. I could handle my own death so much easier than the death of my child. Art prayed over Ashley, we both said our goodbyes, and then with tears streaming down our faces, we let her go.

Art took me outside to the hospital parking lot, where I collapsed into his arms. He gently cupped my face in his hands and reminded me that Ashley was God's child to give and His to take back. "Lysa, God loves Ashley even more than we do," he gently told me. "We must trust His plan."

Art then asked me to do something, and it changed my whole perspective on my relationship with God: "We have to get it settled in our hearts that we will love God no matter the outcome of Ashley's surgery," he said.

At first I resented Art's desire that we love God in this way. I feared it might give Him the impression it was okay to take Ashley. With all my being I wanted to hold on to my child and refuse God. Yet though I felt very heartbroken, I also felt God's compassion. I felt Him drawing me close and pouring out His tender mercy. God knew firsthand the pain we were feeling because He'd felt it Himself. I knew that, ultimately, I had no ability to control my child's future. With tears pouring from our eyes, Art and I released our sweet Ashley to the Lord and promised to love Him no matter what.

That day we settled our love for God not just for this situation but for all time. Though we did not feel at all happy, a gentle covering of unexplainable joy settled over our hearts. Knowing that the One who loved Ashley even more than we did was taking care of her, and that His plan for her was perfect, brought peace in the middle of heartbreak.

The end of this chapter of Ashley's life was miraculous and wonderful. Though the doctors can't explain how,

Ashley made a full recovery. Who can understand why God answers prayers the way He does? We just know we're grateful. And we can also know that no matter God's answer, our hearts were settled to trust and love Him. This kind of radical obedience brings about a depth of relationship with God you can't get any other way.

Job was tested and tried in ways most of us can't imagine. He experienced everything he ever feared: "If only my anguish could be weighed and all my misery be placed on the scales! It would surely outweigh the sand of the seas" (Job 6:2). Even Job's wife said to him, "Are you still holding on to your integrity? Curse God and die!" (Job 2:9). But Job had settled in his heart to trust God: "You are talking like a foolish woman," he told his wife. "Shall we accept good from God, and not trouble?" (Job 2:10). And because of that radical obedience, Job received a radical blessing in his relationship with the Lord: "My ears had heard of you but now my eyes have seen you" (Job 42:5). Job had known of God, but only through his trials and his obedience did he experience God personally.

The psalmist David discovered this radical blessing—this intimate, deep relationship with God—when he settled in his heart to love God no matter what.

> My life is consumed by anguish and
> my years by groaning; my strength fails
> because of my affliction, and my bones
> grow weak…But I trust in you, O LORD;
> I say, "You are my God." My times are in
> your hands; deliver me from my enemies
> and from those who pursue me. Let your
> face shine on your servant; save me in
> your unfailing love…How great is your
> goodness, which you have stored up for
> those who fear you, which you bestow in
> the sight of men on those who take
> refuge in you…Praise be to the LORD, for
> he showed his wonderful love to me
> (Psalm 31:10,14-16,19,21).

With God's amazing love settled in our heart, we have His power to keep our faith steady and to experience lasting hope and joy independent of our situation.

It's true—God wants it all. And it's in the exchange of what we want for what God wants that we experience the adventure and freedom and power of radical obedience.

God is using all of your experiences, both good and bad, to develop your character to match your calling.

After all, dear friend, you *never* know how God will use you until You let Him.

CHAPTER FIVE

WHAT KEEPS US FROM RADICAL OBEDIENCE

Whatever we worship, we will obey.

I could see it in the cross expression on her face and in the urgency in her stride. The woman approaching me had a few things on her mind.

Sure enough, this woman in my Bible study class thought I was taking my faith a little too seriously and the Bible a little too literally. After she dumped her load of concern on me, she smiled and encouraged me to lighten up. "Honey," she said, "I wouldn't want to see you carry this obedience thing too far."

This, my friend, is a naysayer. If you choose the life of radical obedience, you are going to encounter such people. They don't understand you. They don't want to understand you. And often what you're doing makes them feel convicted. If someone is quick to find fault in something good someone else is doing, that person is usually wrapped up in his or her own self-centered outlook. Naysayers make themselves feel better by tearing others down. Paul warned Timothy about people like this:

> But mark this: There will be terrible times in the last days. People will be lovers of themselves, lovers of money, boastful, proud, abusive, disobedient to their parents, ungrateful, unholy, without love, unforgiving, slanderous, without self-control, brutal, not lovers of good, treacherous, rash, conceited, lovers of pleasure rather than lovers of God—having a form of godliness but denying its power. Have nothing to do with them (2 Timothy 3:1).

To be radically obedient is going to cause you to be different from many of your family members and friends. While not all of them will be naysayers, some will. The difference naysayers see in you compels them to come against you full force because Christ working through you steps on the toes of their conscience. While naysayers may talk a good Christian game, they deny Christ in their attitudes and actions toward others. Instead of allowing those feelings of conviction to produce good changes in them, they seek to discourage you in hopes of hushing Christ in you.

It's not easy to keep their negativity from being discouraging, but as my husband always reminds me, "Lysa, consider the source." I ask myself, "Is this person criticizing me active in pursuing a relationship with the Lord? Is this person answering God's call on his life, producing the evidence of Christ's fruit? Does he have my best interest in mind?" The answers are almost always no. So I look for any truth that might be in what this person has said, forgive him for any hurt he may have caused, and let the rest go.

Author Rick Warren, in his book *The Purpose-Driven Life*, comments on naysayers:

> You will find that people who do not understand your shape for ministry will criticize you and try to get you to conform to what they think you should be doing. Ignore them. Paul often had to deal with critics who misunderstood and maligned his service. His response was always the same: Avoid comparisons,

resist exaggerations, and seek only God's commendation.[1]

Rick then goes on to quote John Bunyan as saying, "If my life is fruitless, it doesn't matter who praises me, and if my life is fruitful, it doesn't matter who criticizes me."

That's so true!

The Foes of Grace

Grace for the journey…we all need it. God is the only one we should be living for, and we need His grace to handle the successes and the failures, the applause and the criticism, and everything in between. Sometimes our efforts will be fruitful and other times fruitless. But as long as we please God, it's all for good.

Grace has two fierce foes, though—acceptance and rejection. Imagine, for a moment, a tall, gated wall. Puddles of mud dot the well-worn, barren ground. It is evident that many have lingered here. Two gatekeepers wish to detain you. They wish to take your hand in friendship and have you remain on the outside of the wall. All the while, Jesus is standing on the other side of the wall in an open field full of beauty and adventure. So few have actually made it past the gatekeepers into this field that the blades of grass remain unbroken and the flowers unpicked.

The first gatekeeper is Acceptance. He requires much of me. He seems so enticing with his offerings of compliments and big promises. But though he is fun for a moment, soon my mind is flooded with concerns of being able to continue to impress him. I am quickly overwhelmed with pondering my interactions with others and keeping score on the table of comparison.

The second gatekeeper is Rejection. He also requires much of me. He seems appealing because he gives me permission to excuse myself from following my true calling. Yet he demands that I pull back and shy away from the obedience for which my soul longs. His whispered questions of, "What if?" and "What do they think of you?" linger in my mind and influence my actions and reactions.

How do I deny the lure of these two gatekeepers of grace? After all, I've tasted their laced fruit and, though I'm aware of their poison, I also crave their sweetness. In my flesh I desire the praises of Acceptance and the excuses of Rejection. The limelight of Acceptance shines on the pride that has yet to be driven from my heart. The thought that I am really something eclipses the reality that, but for the grace of Christ, I am nothing. The ease of settling for less is the pull of Rejection. When I listen to him, I shrink back and pull inside myself. I no longer want to press on. I want to quit. The thought that I am really nothing eclipses the reality that, because of the grace of Christ in me, I am a treasured something.

So goes the battle in my heart. Honestly, it sickens me that I even give thought to and feel enticed by these life-draining agents of Satan. Jesus is standing behind these two slick gatekeepers. His arms are open, waiting to embrace and enfold me in the security of His truth. "Hold on to Me and what I say about you," He says. "For my words are the truth of who you are and the essence of what you were created to be." I then imagine Him pausing and, with tears in His eyes and a crack in His voice, He adds, "Then you will know the truth, and the truth will set you free" (John 8:32).

The Great Dance

Pursuing radical obedience has been the most fulfilling adventure I have ever let my heart follow after. However, the journey has not been without bumps and bruises. I would be remiss in this chapter of what keeps us from radical obedience if I did not talk about the great dance between the desire of our flesh and the desire of

God's Spirit in us. Our flesh seeks the approval of others, is swayed by Satan's voice of condemnation, and looks for the comfortable way out. God's Spirit in us opposes Satan and the world's way and offers an unexplainable peace that transcends the circumstances around us.

The dance plays out in rather subtle voices in my head. There is the pull between condemnation and conviction. If I'm hearing thoughts of condemnation, these only come from Satan. There is no condemnation from Jesus, only conviction. It's important for us to know the difference. Condemnation leaves us feeling hopeless and worthless. Conviction invites us to make positive changes in our lives.

I also sometimes find myself getting caught up in my own weariness and grumbling over the empty places of my life. These are all the places that chip away at my contentment, that nag me into thinking I'm being cheated out of something somehow. In my bathroom, for example, I have white tile with green accents and blue-and-white wallpaper. The tile and wallpaper don't really match, and sometimes this bothers me. My car has dings on each of the front doors and a scratch on the driver's side door, and sometimes this bothers me. With all of their great qualities, my kids sometimes pout and whine, and, you guessed it, this bothers me. My husband and I are crazy about each other but still find ways to get on each other's nerves at times, and this bothers me. I struggle with trying to cram too much into too little time and often find myself running late—which really bothers me. These little things get piled on top of bigger things, and I can really get down.

There are things in my life, little and big, that fall short, don't meet my expectations, and cause grumpy feelings inside my heart. Do you ever sense empty places in your life too? *Yes.*

Usually this happens to me when the busyness of life has crowded out my quiet times with Jesus. When I have not spent enough time allowing the Lord to refuel and refill me, I forget that this is not my real home. When my soul gets down, these places can be distracting and difficult. And sometimes the reality is we feel hurt and discouraged.

The Choice to Worry or Worship

It is when we find ourselves in these hard places that we make the choice to worry or worship. When we worry, we feel we have to come up with justifications and careful explanations for the naysayers. When we worry, we listen to the voices of Acceptance and Rejection. When we worry, we lay awake at night and ponder Satan's lies. When we worry, we have pity parties where the guests of honor are Negative Thinking, Doubt, and Resignation.

But we can make the choice to worship. When we worship in these hard places, we are reminded that none of this is about us—it is all about God. We turn our focus off of ourselves and back onto God Almighty. God can use empty places in your life to draw your heart to Him. He is the great love of your life who will never disappoint. He is building your eternal home that will never get broken, dirty, or need redecorating. He is preparing a place of eternal perfect fellowship where no one will be a naysayer. And heaven won't be limited to human time-frames, so no one will ever be late...not even me!

Our hearts were made for perfection in the Garden of Eden, but the minute sin came into the picture, strokes of imperfection began to cast a dingy hue. When we know Christ, however, we know this is not all there is. Realizing that this life is temporary helps me to live beyond this moment and rejoice in what is to come. Each time I feel my heart being pulled down into the pit of ungrate-fulness and grumbling, I recognize it as a call to draw near to the Lord. I thank Him for the empty places, for they remind me that only He has the ability to fill me com-pletely. In my worship of Him, my soul is safe and comforted and reassured and at peace.

We all worship something. We must choose whom—or what—we will worship. Will it be the opinions of others, our fears, or even our own comfort? Or will it be the One who created our souls to worship? Whatever we worship, we will obey. As we choose to be radically obedient to the Lord, we must be radical about choosing to worship Him and Him alone.

Peace like a River

And what is the result of choosing to worship God, to obey Him alone? "Peace is the fruit of the obedient, righteous life."[2] If I am ever going to find peace past the naysayers, past the attacks of Satan, and past my own weariness, it will only be because I choose daily to walk in absolute obedience to the moment-by-moment, day-by-day, assignment-by-assignment commands of the Lord.

The prophet Isaiah writes, "If only you had paid attention to my commands, your peace would have been like a river, your righteousness like the waves of the sea" (Isaiah 48:18). Did you catch the treasure hidden here? One of the most radical blessings for the radically obedient is the peace that rushes through the soul of the one who is attentive to the Lord's commands.

God chose such a unique word to describe His peace—a river! A river is not calm and void of activity. It is active and cleansing and very confident of the direction it is headed. It also doesn't get caught up with the rocks that are in its path. It flows over and around them, all the while smoothing their jagged edges and allowing them to add to its beauty rather than take away from it. A river is a wonderful thing to behold. Beth Moore says, "To have peace like a river is to have security and tranquility while meeting the many bumps and unexpected turns on life's journey. Peace is submission to a trustworthy Authority, not resignation from activity."[3]

Jesus tells us His peace is unlike the world's peace: "Peace I leave with you; my peace I give you. I do not give to you as the world gives. Do not let your hearts be troubled and do not be afraid" (John 14:27). The world's way to peace would have me pull back to make life a little easier for me, my circumstances, my family. The problem with this is that we were not put here to be all about ourselves—we were put here to be all about God. We are to die to our self-centeredness so we can have more of Christ in our hearts and minds. Jesus clearly tells us to focus on Him, His ways, and His example, and His peace will be with us. The focus of our hearts and minds will shape our decisions and actions that follow: "You [God] will keep in perfect peace him whose mind is steadfast, because he trusts in you" (Isaiah 26:3).

When we focus our minds and fix our attention on Christ and Christ alone, He is magnified and made bigger in our lives. When we focus our minds and fix our attention on life's obstacles, they will be wrongly magnified and made to appear larger than they really are. Our attention is like a magnifying glass—whatever we place it on becomes larger and more consuming of our time and energy. We desire to focus on Christ alone, but sometimes other things seem bigger, and so, without even realizing it, we shift our focus: "For the sinful nature desires what is contrary to the Spirit, and the Spirit what is contrary to the sinful nature. They are in conflict with each other, so that you do not do what you want" (Galatians 5:17). Before we know it, we are drawn into the muck and mire on the outer banks of Jesus' river of peace.

But sometimes it is down on your face in the mud in complete humility (and sometimes even humiliation!) that you will find a sweet and tender truth. It's from this position that you can say, "Jesus, I love You and want You more than anything else. I love You and want You more than the approval of my peers and even the naysayers in my life. I love You and want You more than the comforts and trappings of this world. I love You and choose to believe Your truth over Satan's lies. I love You and choose to worship You and You alone. Jesus, I love You and want to come to You empty-handed and offer my life in complete surrender."

Radical obedience is choosing who I will worship and then depending on God to give me the strength to follow through. As my soul looks up from life's muck and rights the focus of its attention, I find myself pressing back into the river, where Jesus' peace rushes over me, refreshing, cleansing, and invigorating.

CHAPTER SIX

IF IT WERE EASY, IT WOULDN'T BE WORTH DOING

Radical obedience is born out of delight, not duty.

I was discouraged. In two months' time my life went from being wonderfully fulfilling and clicking right along to completely topsy-turvy. I felt myself getting caught in a whirlwind of emotions. My computer went on the blink and some very important documents disappeared. A big book deal I was very excited about fell through. Our well broke, and we had to go several days without water. A diamond fell out of my wedding ring.

Then on top of a host of other interruptions and haphazard happenings, my husband blew out his knee and had to have major reconstructive surgery, leaving him bedridden for nearly five weeks. I didn't know whether to laugh or cry. A friend of mine hit the nail on the head when she said, "Lysa, I think when you go with God to a new level you get a new devil."

While I'm not sure about the exact theological correctness to that statement, I do know that Satan hates the radically obedient soul. He hates it when a person jumps off the fence of complacency and into the center of God's will. There is a spiritual battle raging around us and, because of that, life is hard. While radical obedience brings radical blessing, it is not easy. So, if our desire for radical obedience is born merely out of duty, we may be quick to give up. However, if our desire is born out of delight, out of a love relationship that burns deep in our soul, it won't be extinguished—no matter the cost.

Purpose, Perspective, Persistence

One of my favorite love stories in the Bible is that of Jacob and Rachel. Jacob's love for Rachel gave him purpose and perspective which led to amazing persistence. He served Rachel's father for many years to earn the right to marry Rachel because he loved her that much: "So Jacob served seven years to get Rachel, but they seemed like only a few days to him because of his love for her" (Genesis 29:20).

Do you see what love can do for a person's view of his circumstances? When you are crazy in love with someone, you'll do anything for him—and do it with the highest level of sheer joy. I want to be so crazy in love with Jesus that not only do I serve Him, but I do it with absolute delight.

A real sign of spiritual maturity is looking to God not for comfort and convenience but for purpose and perspective. Comfort and convenience lead to complacency. When trouble comes, the complacent person becomes critical of everyone, including God. On the other hand, purpose and perspective lead to the perseverance that is evident in those living a truly devoted life. The persistent person eagerly looks to handle trials and struggles in a way that honors God and allows personal growth.

Because we love God, we look for and trust in His purpose in everything. The persistent person understands the meaning of Romans 8:28: "And we know that in all things God works for the good of those that love him, who have been called according to his purpose." This does not mean that everything that happens to us will be good but that God will work in and through every situation to bring good from it. And let's not miss the last four words of this verse, where we are reminded that it is all "according to His purpose." God has a purpose, and His plans to accomplish that purpose are perfect. Trusting God's good purpose, and seeking to understand that He takes all the events from our life and orchestrates good from them, leads to a changed perspective.

Seeing God in Everything

Our changed perspective helps us see God in everything. I am convinced that Satan wants to keep my perspective in a place where my heart is discouraged and my mind is questioning God. Yet God's Word calls me to a different action: "Not only so, but we also rejoice in our sufferings, because we know that suffering produces perseverance; perseverance, character; and character, hope" (Romans 5:3). God's Word calls me to rejoice! Not that I rejoice in the bad things—I would have to fake that. But I *can* rejoice in what God is doing in me through difficult times.

When Art hurt his knee, we prayed and prayed that this would be a minor injury and surgery wouldn't be required. We just knew that God was going to go before us and make the way smooth for this injury. However, when the test results came back, we were facing a worst-case scenario. Not only would Art have to have surgery, but it was one of the worst knee injuries the doctor had ever seen. Simply looking at the circumstances and the doctor's report, we might have been tempted to get pulled into Satan's lies that God had not answered our prayers, that He wasn't trustworthy. However, the truth is that God is faithful and true, and His Word promises us, "For he has not despised or disdained the suffering of the afflicted one; he has not hidden his face from him but listened to his cry for help" (Psalm 22:24).

So what do we do with the fact that my very athletic husband is out of commission for several months? What does he do about missing many weeks of work and having his life totally interrupted? What do I do with my feelings of being overwhelmed and frustrated because I have three small children with whom I need his help? What do I do with the fact that he can't drive, is in extreme pain, and needs my unconditional love and support—even on the days when I'm too tired to give it?

Okay, God, where are You? I cried out. There were too many details and too much stress. Our everyday life was already too busy, and now this. To be completely honest, I started to get a little frustrated with God. Satan was having a field day.

Provision, Protection, Process

What do you do when you feel as though God isn't hearing your cries for help? Or, worse yet, He's saying no?

It hasn't been easy, and God has had to remind me several times, but here's what I do know: God *always* hears me when I cry out to Him, and when He says no, it's for my provision, my protection, and it's part of the process of growing me more like Christ.

Provision

On one of my "Woe is me, my husband is still in bed and I am still doing everything" days, I took my three kids along with a friend's child out to lunch. I was determined to have a good attitude, but with each whiney response and sibling spat I could feel my blood pressure rising. I was at the counter trying to place my order and keep an eye on the kids sitting in the booth across the restaurant when a lady came up and put her hand gently on my shoulder. "I've got your napkins and straws," she said, "and I'll put them on your table." I was shocked. Who was this sweet stranger?

After I made my way back to my table, I found her sitting with her family and went over to thank her. When I did, she told me that when I walked into the restaurant, God told her to help me. She didn't know who I was until I turned around to talk to her at the counter, and she recognized me as the speaker from a women's conference she attended last spring. She then went on to ask me if she could make my family a meal. I told her that my husband had just had surgery and a meal would be great.

I walked back to my booth with tears in my eyes. Just that morning I had cried out to God to fill in the gaps where I was feeling weary and weak. I asked Him to be my portion of all I needed to take care of my family that day. God was answering my prayer! My perspective totally changed. God was working good from Art's surgery. He had said no to us not having to have surgery, but He didn't leave us in that hard spot. He was teaching us about His provision.

How can He be our Ultimate Provider if we aren't ever lacking and in need? I was so touched by this lady's obedience to God's call to reach out to me. I was blown away by the personal and practical way God answered my cries for help despite my bad attitude.

Protection

My husband is an avid runner and can often be seen running the country roads near our home. After his knee injury occurred, he was very disappointed, to say the least, when the doctor told him it could be up to a year before he could run again—and that some people with this type of injury have to give up running altogether. Anytime we have to take a break from something we really enjoy, it is hard. But the thought of forever giving up running seemed too much to swallow.

Then came the call from a friend who knew of a man who was injured playing flag football the same week that Art had been injured, only the doctors were telling him he would never walk again. He was now paralyzed from the waist down for life. Then another call came from a friend who told me she read in the paper of a man riding his bike on the same roads my husband runs on. This man was struck by a car and killed.

Art and I had been so quick to throw a pity party over our circumstances, but now we were coming to the realization that God had protected him from situations that could have been a lot worse.

I confess I don't always understand the ways of God in these circumstances—why Art would just need surgery while another man lay paralyzed and another man was killed. Many have had to go through severe circumstances and unfathomable pain, and my own family is no exception. We have experienced tragedy. But I know that I know that I know: God has worked good in every one of these situations. As I look back and reflect on our difficult times, I can see how He has protected us.

Part of the Process

Ultimately, our time here on earth is for one single purpose: to grow more and more like Christ. Each of us comes to a place in our Christian journey where we have to make the decision whether we will become part of that process or not. I wrote a poem to express that moment of decision:

A man journeyed to a place
Where the road caused him to ponder,
Should he travel the wide, clear road?
Or should he venture up the other?

The wide road was more often traveled,
It was level and easy and clear.
The narrow one seemed barely a path,
With very few footprints there.

His senses said to choose for ease
And walk where many have wandered.
But the map he held in his hand
Showed the narrow going somewhere grander.

In life we will all come to a point
Where a decision must be made.
Will we choose to walk with comfort's guide?
Or journey the narrow path God says?

We want to live the totally sold-out life for Christ, yet there are other things pulling at us, enticing us, calling out to us—causing our indecision. Brent Curtis and John Eldredge said it well in their book *The Sacred Romance:*

> At some point on our Christian journey, we all stand at the edge of those geographies where our heart has been satisfied by less-wild lovers, whether they be those of competence and order or those of indulgence. If we listen to our heart again, perhaps for the first time in a while, it tells us how weary it is of the familiar and indulgent. We find ourselves once again at the intersection with the road that is the way of the heart. We look down it once more and see what appears to be a looming abyss between the lovers we have known and the mysterious call of Christ.[1]

In times where the road diverges in front of us, we can either fall away from God or fall toward Him. During Art's long healing process he made the decision to fall toward God and humbly thank Him for allowing the injury to happen. He chose to look for opportunities every day to rejoice in this trial and make the most of being still and quiet. He dove into God's Word and spent hours praying, reading, and writing notes about all God was teaching him.

Christmas happened to fall right in the middle of Art's recovery. Every Christmas morning we have a special breakfast with Jesus where we give Him a gift from our heart. I wondered what gift Art would have this year. When his turn came, he said he wanted to look for a way to serve another or give to another in Christ's name every day for the next year. By next Christmas he will know that 365 people's lives were made better because of Christ in him. My sweet husband made a choice to rejoice in the process of growing more like Christ, and what a difference it made not only in his life but in others' lives as well.

The prophet Jeremiah wrote, "Because of the LORD's great love we are not consumed, for his compassions never fail. They are new every morning; great is your faithfulness. I say to myself, 'The Lord is my portion; therefore I will wait for him' " (Lamentations 3:22-24). God is our portion of protection and peace. He's our portion of provision and security. He's our portion of all of the joy and patience we need during the process of growing more like

Christ. He is our portion of whatever we need, whenever we need it—if only we'll recall His goodness and ask Him.

It isn't going to be easy. But we have Jesus and His power, and that power is able to completely change our outlook on life. This is how we can find the kind of joy the apostle Peter talks about: "Though you have not seen him, you love him; and even though you do not see him now, you believe in him and are filled with an inexpressible and glorious joy" (1 Peter 1:8). This is a radical blessing for the radically obedient—the ability to have a radically different perspective.

We're human. We know we're not always going to like our circumstances. But we can choose to find the joy in all things, and we can expect God to show up and be our daily portion of everything we need. It's a radical obedience born out of delight, not duty.

CHAPTER SEVEN

KEEPING OUR VISION CLEAR

Our life will follow where we focus our vision.

My husband and I found ourselves blessed with a little extra money once, and I started dreaming of new kitchen curtains. I stood in the kitchen and envisioned beautiful toile fabric cascading down and around my windows. I was so excited. I pleaded with my less-than-enthusiastic-about-the-curtains husband to understand that a woman's home is an expression of who she is, that curtains were important to the overall happiness I felt in my home. I even went so far as to pull out some handy-dandy Scriptures straight from Proverbs 31! I showed Art how this biblical woman made coverings for her bed, and I was sure she made matching window treatments as well.

Art still wasn't convinced. He kept gently telling me he felt led to give the money to ministry.

Ministry! Our whole lives were dedicated to ministry! "Honey," I countered, "I will have so much more to offer if only I feel complete and refreshed in our home. Did I mention that the home is the way a woman expresses her God-given creativity?"

My arguments, however, were not working. Eventually, my countenance turned sour and my words turned cold and flat toward my husband.

"Look, Lysa," Art finally said, exasperated, "if it's that big of a deal, we'll get the curtains."

I had won! You'd think I'd be overcome with joy and glee, but I caught a glimpse of my face in our bathroom mirror. It wasn't happy. It was harsh and pinched. I wasn't about to be deterred, though. I just needed a little makeup and all would be well. I reached underneath my sink where I keep my makeup bag, and it was gone. Then I felt God speak to my heart. He told me no amount of makeup was going to help what was wrong with me, and He would not allow me to find my makeup until I got back on track.

What? I asked Him in disbelief. *Don't You have some terrorists to round up? Or some hardened criminal to convict?* It was ridiculous to think that God would hide my makeup, so I determined to prove how crazy this was by finding my bag. I searched the entire house and both of our cars. I looked high and I looked low, and my make-up was nowhere to be found.

During my great hide-and-seek game, I continued to hear God's still small voice speaking to me. As He tugged and prodded and convicted, I came to realize that my harsh facial expression was reflective of something ugly in my heart. My desire about what to do with the money had been all about me, me, me! Never once did I stop to pray. Instead, I pushed on with my agenda. Never once did I stop to consider the beautiful thing God was doing in my husband's heart by giving him the desire to share more abundantly. Never once did I take a step back to consider God's bigger picture and plan.

Was there anything wrong with new curtains? No. Was there anything wrong with my heart? Oh, yes. I had closed my heart to what God wanted, to His calling. I had limited my vision to new curtains and, had it stayed there, that's all I may have been blessed with. But if I took hold of His vision, the Lord gently reminded me, how much more would my life be blessed?

That night, when Art came in from work, I humbly went before him and told him how wrong it was that I had been so self-centered. With tears in my eyes, I apologized for not stopping long enough to consider what he and God wanted. Art accepted my apology, and suddenly I knew where my makeup was. Even though I had already thoroughly searched Art's car, I asked if he would go look once more. When he did, he found the makeup bag on the passenger floorboard—in plain sight.

God's Bigger, Grander Vision

Why is it that we can be so nearsighted when it comes to God's plans for us? Why do we let what's right in front of us distract us from the bigger, grander vision God has in mind?

To be radically obedient is to keep God's vision clearly in front of us, to be so busy looking at what He wants, looking at *Him*, that everything else becomes less important. C.S. Lewis describes it as looking at "something beyond":

> I think all Christians would agree with me if I said that though Christianity seems at first to be all about morality, all about duties and guilt and virtue, yet it leads you on, out of all of that, into something beyond. One has a glimpse of a country where they do not talk of those things, except perhaps as a joke. Everyone there is filled with light. But they do not call it goodness. They do not call it anything. They are not thinking of it. They

are too busy looking for the source from which it comes.[1]

Oh, Lord, give me the desire to be too busy looking at You to consider anything but Your plan! Strip away my short and narrow vision to see the wonderful adventure of truly being Your follower. Help me to be like Your disciples who followed immediately and fully rather than the people who simply played games at the foot of Your cross.

True Disciples vs. the Game Players

Two New Testament accounts from the life of Jesus contrast the true disciples from the game players. First, we find Simon Peter.

> He [Jesus] saw at the water's edge two boats, left there by the fishermen, who were washing their nets. He got into one of the boats, the one belonging to Simon, and asked him to put out a little from shore. Then he sat down and taught the people from the boat. When he had finished speaking, he said to Simon, "Put out into deep water, and let down the nets for a catch" (Luke 5:2-4).

Did you notice that there were two boats on the shore that day, and Jesus specifically chose Simon Peter's boat? Why? Because Jesus knew Simon Peter had a radically obedient heart and would be willing to do what He asked him—even when it made no sense. I like Peter's response to Jesus' request: "Master, we've worked hard all night and haven't caught anything. But because you say so, I will let down the nets" (verse 5). Do you hear what Peter is saying? "Though I'm tired from working all night, though I don't think You know much about fishing, Jesus, though it makes no sense at all in human terms…because You say so, I will do it."

How many times have I found myself in Peter's position and *not* responded in obedience the way he did? It saddens my heart to remember the occasions I've ignored Jesus' call for my radical obedience because I was tired, or because I didn't really believe Jesus would work miraculously in a particular situation, or mostly because the Lord's request made no sense in human terms.

I often wonder now at the blessings I've missed because of my lack of obedience. Look at what happened to Peter because of his obedience:

> When they had [let the nets down],
> they caught such a large number of fish
> that their nets began to break. So they

> signaled their partners in the other boat
> to come and help them, and they came
> and filled both boats so full that they
> began to sink. When Simon Peter saw this,
> he fell at Jesus' knees and said, "Go away
> from me, Lord; I am a sinful man!" For
> he and all his companions were aston-
> ished at the catch of fish they had taken,
> and so were James and John, the sons of
> Zebedee, Simon's partners (Luke 5:6-10).

But Simon Peter's blessing that day didn't end with a huge catch of fish. His radical obedience to Jesus' simple request ultimately resulted in him discovering the calling on his life.

> Then Jesus said to Simon, "Don't be
> afraid; from now on you will catch men."
> So they pulled their boats up on shore,
> left everything and followed him (Luke
> 5:10-11).

We have to remember that Simon Peter didn't know that something as mundane as lowering his net into the water would change his life—but it did! And that's how it can be for us. Our calling is revealed as we walk in daily obedience to Christ in the little things.

That's what's remarkable about radical obedience. You don't know where it will lead. You don't know how God will use it. That's what I love about Peter's story. It shows us so much about the radically obedient life.

First, as Peter discovered, *our call to obedience may challenge our pride.* God hates a prideful attitude (James 4:6). Many times the little steps leading to the bigger steps in our calling will be tests that help whittle the pride out of our heart. Peter, for instance, could have easily questioned Jesus' fishing knowledge...after all, Peter was a professional fisherman and Jesus was a carpenter. But Peter chose to swallow his pride and take the small step of obedience.

Second, *God uses our experiences to equip us for our calling.* God doesn't waste our experiences in life. I know in my own life God has been able to weave everything together to form a beautiful tapestry of good experiences, bad experiences, hurtful things, joyous things, professional jobs, ministry jobs, and everything else to prepare me for the work He is in the process of revealing to me. The same was true for Simon Peter. Yesterday he was fishing for fish; today he would be fishing for men.

Third, *our obedience may inspire others to respond.* What a radical blessing! As we respond in obedience, others will catch the vision and respond to God's calling on their own lives. Think of it. It wasn't just Peter's life that changed that day. The lives of his fishing partners, James and John, were never the same either. And it started with Peter saying yes to Jesus.

One caution at this point. We need to be careful not to fall into the trap of thinking that our blessings for radical obedience will profit our accounts and fill our pockets. Yes, Peter got a boatload of fish as a result of his obedience, but notice what he did: "So they pulled their boats up on shore, left everything and followed him" (Luke 5:11). They didn't celebrate their banner fishing day. They didn't consider the fish a just reward for all their hard work. They didn't sell the fish and use the money to buy more boats and hang out a new shingle announcing their expanded fishing fleet. No, they were only thinking of the person who allowed it to happen—and they left it all behind and followed Him. Sounds a lot like that C.S. Lewis quote, "They do not call it anything. They are not thinking of it. They are too busy looking for the source from which it comes."

Where We Focus Our Vision

Now contrast Peter's story with another incident we find recorded in Luke:

Jesus said, "Father, forgive them, for they do not know what they are doing." And they divided up his clothes by casting lots (Luke 23:34).

It's hard to imagine anyone playing games in the shadow of the cross while the Savior of the world looked on in excruciating pain. He was dying for their sins, and they were dying for one good roll of the dice. They didn't even hear His cry for God to forgive them. They missed His offer of eternal significance because they were too distracted by earthly rags. They had no vision beyond the moment. Max Lucado writes of this scene:

It makes me think of us...I'm thinking that we are not so unlike those soldiers. We, too, play games at the foot of the cross. We compete for members. We scramble for status. We deal out judgments and condemnations. Competition. Selfishness. Personal gain. It's all there...So close to the timber yet so far from the blood.[2]

So, are we like Peter? Or are we like these soldiers at the foot of the cross? Our life will follow where we choose to focus our vision. If we are serious about radical obedience, about having a vision that's God inspired, then we must keep our focus on Christ. When Christ speaks, we must listen. When He directs us to act, we must act. When He compels us to give, we must do so freely. When He reminds us to get past trivial matters, we must let our pride fall away. When He invites us to leave the world behind, we must follow Him.

For Peter, it was a net full of fish. For me, it was those kitchen curtains. Would I still like new kitchen curtains? Sure. But I've decided I won't be distracted by wanting them more than wanting the Lord's vision. I'm going to be too busy keeping my eyes on the "source," on Jesus Himself, to notice what's hanging in my windows.

CHAPTER EIGHT

GIVING UP WHAT WAS NEVER OURS

We are managers, not owners, of God's resources.

I was going through a fast food drive-through one day when I realized I didn't have enough cash on me to pay for the lunch I'd ordered for my daughter Hope and myself. I knew Hope, who had just celebrated her ninth birthday, had received a ten-dollar bill as a gift from her aunt. I asked Hope if I could borrow just a few dollars to make up for my shortage, and I promised I would pay her back. She refused, explaining that she was seeing some of her friends that afternoon and wanted to show them her ten-dollar bill. It just would not be the same to show them a five-dollar bill and a couple of ones. No, she insisted, she had to keep her ten-dollar bill for herself.

I asked her if she trusted that I would pay her back. She said she did, but I might not pay her back with a ten-dollar bill. She did not want two fives. She did not want ten ones. She did not want any combination of bills. She wanted a ten. A ten-dollar bill would, after all, be much more impressive to her friends.

As it was approaching my turn at the drive-through window, I got more aggressive with my offer. I told her I would not only give her the change from her original ten-dollar bill, which was going to be about seven dollars, but that I would also give her another ten-dollar bill later. Even this offer was not enough to release her tight grip on her beloved bill. She did not want a ten-dollar bill later because she might miss showing off to her friends today.

Did my sweet daughter not realize that I had the ability to bless her with many ten-dollar bills? Did she not appreciate the fact that I had just spent the equivalent of more than ten ten-dollar bills on her birthday party? Did she even have a clue of how many ten-dollar bills I've spent on her over her lifetime? Not to mention the fact that her lunch was part of the reason I was spending this ten-dollar bill at the moment?

Finally, when we were at the window, Hope begrudgingly gave me the money. How it disappointed me that she would not willingly release the ten-dollar bill.

How it must disappoint God when we do this very same thing.

You see, I had special knowledge that Hope did not have. I knew that waiting in our mailbox at home was another birthday card—one from her grandmother that contained a whopping fifty dollars! Her ten-dollar bill would pale in comparison.

Likewise, God has special knowledge in our lives. He has blessings for the radically obedient that make the dime-store stuff we are so intent on holding onto pale in comparison. The question is do we trust Him? Do we trust that He will bless us? Do we trust that His blessings are infinitely better than what He might first ask us to release?

The Floodgates of Blessing

Trust. Isn't that why more of us don't offer all we have to God? We don't trust that He really will throw open the floodgates of blessing in return.

> "Bring the whole tithe into the storehouse, that there may be food in my house. Test me in this," says the LORD Almighty, "and see if I will not throw open the floodgates of heaven and pour out so

much blessing that you will not have room enough for it" (Malachi 3:10).

Sacrificial giving is one of the few times that God asks us to test Him. Yet for many years I found myself unwilling to accept the challenge. I was willing to tithe but not willing to go beyond what I felt comfortable giving. Leaving our comfort zone, however, is the very place God calls us to. He wants us to venture into truly abundant giving. He wants us to get out from under our own selfishness with our possessions and accept His invitation to become radically obedient with what we own. Then, not only will He bless us, but He will lavish blessing upon blessing on us.

I saw this firsthand when I was saving money for a new outfit. I started this "new outfit fund" because of an embarrassing situation I found myself in during a country club speaking engagement. I was wearing what I thought was a very nice outfit. When I showed up at the event, however, I quickly realized that not only was my outfit a little out of style but my white discount store shoes were the only light-colored foot apparel in the entire building. (Not being a queen of fashion, I was unaware of the rule that white shoes have to wait until after Memorial Day in some parts of the country.) Everyone had on dark-colored shoes, so with very step I took, I felt as though my feet were screaming, "White shoes! Everyone look at my shocking white shoes!"

You'll be happy to know that not even white shoes could stop me from sharing about Jesus with this lovely group of women, but you better believe I was determined to update and improve my wardrobe.

It took me a while, but I managed to save up one hundred dollars in my "new outfit fund," so I set a date to go shopping with some of my fashion-savvy friends. Just a few days before I was to go shopping, another dear friend phoned to ask me to pray for her family's financial situation. They could not make ends meet and had many bills they were unable to pay. She mentioned they needed one hundred dollars immediately. While she was only asking me to pray for her and nothing more, I knew God was looking for a response from me that would honor Him. I prayed for my friend and I obeyed God's prompting to give to her the money I'd saved.

The day arrived for my shopping trip, and I must admit that instead of being excited, I felt a pang of dread. I knew that because I had given my money away, I could only look and not purchase anything. I didn't want my fashion friends to think I was wasting their time, so I decided I would put whatever clothes they picked out for me on hold and pray that God would provide the means to return later and purchase them.

While I was moping about and strategizing, God was at work in my fashion friends' hearts. After trying on three beautiful outfits complete with shoes and accessories, I returned to my dressing room to try and decide which outfit to put on hold. While I dressed, my friends took everything to the checkout counter and treated me to a $700 shopping spree!

"Test me in this," says the Lord Almighty, "and see if I will not throw open the floodgates of heaven and pour out so much blessing that you will not have room for it." I was shocked and humbled that God had taken the little gift I'd given to my friend and returned it sevenfold through my other friends.

The Life That Is Truly Life

The apostle Paul wrote:

> Command those who are rich in this present world not to be arrogant nor to put their hope in wealth, which is so uncertain, but to put their hope in God, who richly provides us with everything for our enjoyment. Command them to

do good, to be rich in good deeds, and to be generous and willing to share. In this way they will lay up treasure for themselves as a firm foundation for the coming age, so that they may take hold of the life that is truly life (1 Timothy 6:17-19).

In this country, I think we would agree that most of us are "rich" and this passage applies to us. So, what motivates us to venture out into the area of sacrificial giving—an area that for many of us is a real stretch? There are two radical blessings tucked within Paul's words here. The first, which is also referenced in Matthew 6, speaks of laying up treasures in heaven—sending that which we cannot take with us ahead where we can enjoy it and benefit from it in eternity. If you knew you could immediately enjoy a treasure for one day or enjoy it forever if you waited just a short while, which would you choose? In this light, the eternal route makes so much more sense.

The second blessing goes hand in hand with the first. God is aware of our humanness and our desire for instant gratification. He tends to that as well. Not only are we blessed for eternity when we give, but we are blessed for today too: *So that they may take hold of the life that is truly life.* To live life that is "truly life" is to live abundantly in the here and now.

In his book *The Treasure Principle,* Randy Alcorn wrote:

> The act of giving is a vivid reminder that it's all about God, not about us. It's saying I am not the point, *He* is the point. He does not exist for me. I exist for Him. God's money has a higher purpose than my affluence. Giving is a joyful surrender to a greater person and a greater agenda. Giving affirms Christ's lordship. It dethrones me and exalts Him. It breaks the chains of mammon that would enslave me. As long as I still have something, I believe I own it. But when I give it away, I relinquish control, power and prestige. At the moment of release the light turns on. The magic spell is broken. My mind clears. I recognize God as owner, myself as servant, and others as intended beneficiaries of what God has entrusted to me.[1]

If we choose to obey and give of our resources in abundance, a feeling of amazing satisfaction will follow. The radical blessing of being able to take hold of a real life—a fulfilled and satisfied life we can't find any other way—will be ours.

Seeing Beyond Our Own Mailbox

I must admit that sometimes I am tempted to become consumed with all the ministry opportunities just within the walls of the TerKeurst home. Homeschooling two elementary-aged daughters while keeping our preschool-aged daughter out of trouble can be a delightful but daunting task at times. Yet while my family is my primary ministry, it is not my only ministry.

God has placed the desire in my heart to reach out past my mailbox, past myself, and look for opportunities to live a sacrificial life that touches others for Christ. Sometimes these others are complete strangers whom I touch for a moment and pray God will use me to draw their hearts closer to Him. Other times the opportunities I'm blessed with are with people I know and come in contact with often enough to see God's bigger plan after I play my small role. Such was the case with my dear friend Genia one evening as we gathered with a couple of our close friends for dinner.

Genia and I are part of a small group of very close friends. We call our group "ASAP," which stands for Accountability, Sharing our dreams, Asking the tough questions, and Praying for one another. One night during our meeting, Genia was sharing a tough place she found herself in. As she described her situation, it reminded me of a song on my favorite CD. The Christian artist who sang the song perfectly described what it is like to be caught between life before really living for Christ and life where you sense God leading. This longing to go back and yet the desire to move ahead into a deeper walk with Christ was the place my friend found herself. I knew I had to let Genia hear this song.

After dinner I asked Genia to walk to my car with me to listen to the CD. I was in the process of telling her how I had this CD on continual play in my car because I loved it so much when God interrupted my thoughts and told me to give Genia the CD.

As the song played, Genia had tears in her eyes and told me that it perfectly described how she was feeling. I pushed eject, placed the CD in its plastic case, and handed it to her. I told her that God wanted her to have this CD, so now it was hers. Instead of listening to the music as I made my way home that night, I sat in silent prayer for my friend. It was a beautiful ride home.

The next day, Genia called with such excitement in her voice that she could hardly contain herself. She said she had listened to the CD over and over. She had played it for her husband, who agreed it perfectly described their situation. Then she remembered something that brought her to her knees. Three weeks earlier she'd attended a special prayer service where a woman whom Genia did not know came over and prayed with her. The woman told Genia that God loved her, He understood where she was, He promised not to leave her, and that He would give her a song to minister to her. "A song, Lysa, a song!" she exclaimed. "God promised me a song, and He used your hands to deliver it last night."

Tears welled up in my eyes as I realized what I thought was a simple gift had actually been a well-timed God event for my friend's life! But the blessing didn't end there. Later that same day, the vice president of a large ministry called me on my cell phone. She said God had given her an idea for special retreats to reach women all across the country. She told God that she would write down any names that came to her mind as possible leaders for these retreats. She took out a piece of paper and instantly three names came to mind. She wrote her own name at the top. She then wrote two other names that had really been on her heart: mine and the Christian artist of the CD I had given to Genia.

All I did was give away a CD.

The Blessings of a Sacrificial Life

Understanding and discovering the beautiful opportunities of sacrificial living is so opposite of what the world tells us, and yet it is the only way to find the happiness and joy our hearts long for. The apostle John put it this way:

> Dear children, let us not love with words or tongue but with actions and in truth. This then is how we know that we belong to the truth, and how we set our hearts at rest in his presence (1 John 3:18-19).

I am convinced there is a treasure in life that very few find: a heart that is at rest in His presence. And how do we find this heart at rest? Through actions and in truth. I must confess I have moments where my heart is at rest in His presence, but they are broken up by pitfalls and pity parties. Sometimes I just simply want to be selfish. But when I choose selfishness, I may be happy for the moment but I'm miserable in the long run.

Yet, my Lord with His incredible patience doesn't leave me in my misery. I call out to Him in repentance and, just like a connect-the-dots game, Jesus fills in the gaps between the dots to reveal a beautiful picture of Himself in my life. What if there were less and less space between my dots, revealing an even clearer picture of Christ in my life at all times? Oh, that it could be so. If only I could learn to practice the presence of Christ at every moment, in every decision, with all whom I come in contact. Setting my heart at rest in His presence in this way comes with practice and maturity. The more I practice His presence, the more I will experience His presence, and the more mature I will become.

Elizabeth George talks about the process of maturity in a beautiful way:

> The Old Testament term for the word gentleness, *anah*, describes a mature, ripened shock of grain with its head bent low and bowed down. Just think for a moment on the beauty of this word picture. As wheat grows, the young sprouts rise above the rest. Their heads shoot up

the highest because no grain has yet formed. In their immaturity, little fruit, if any, has appeared. But, as time passes and maturity sets in, fruit comes forth— so much of it that the burdened stalk bends and its head sinks lower and lower —and the lower the head the greater amount of fruit.[2]

Lord, help me to lower my head past my selfishness and pride, past desiring others to serve me and onto serving others, past wanting more and onto giving more, past me in search of You. Help me to always desire the lowered head, full of Your fruit and consumed with Your presence. Help me to be forever mindful of my ministry at home as well as the ministry opportunities that wait beyond my own mailbox.

God owns it all. We are simply managers of His resources. When we pursue the beautiful opportunities of sacrificial living, we freely acknowledge that truth and then reap the blessings. When we come to understand that we're giving up what was never ours to begin with, we're walking in radical obedience.

CHAPTER NINE

RADICALLY BLESSED

The blessings of radical obedience are unending.

The other day, I was driving down a busy road when I came upon a traffic light that was both green and red at the same time. I slowed, unsure of what I should do, as did the other cars coming from all directions. It was confusing and dangerous. Some people stopped, others ran right through the light, and still others pulled off to the side of the intersection.

I finally made it through the intersection and thought about this unusual happening. It was as if God were showing me a visual picture of what it's like when a person is indecisive in her obedience to Him. We can't seek to follow God wholeheartedly if part of our heart is being pulled in a different direction. We can't pursue the radically obedient life and still continue to flirt with disobedience in certain areas of our life. We can't be both red and green toward God at the same time. It gets us nowhere. It's confusing. It's dangerous.

This book has been your invitation to become radically obedient and radically blessed, and now it's time to respond.

Don't be afraid, my friend. I know your mind might be flooded with the same questions that flooded my mind as I was responding to this invitation.

"What if I don't feel able to make such a commitment?"

"What if I say yes and then mess up?"

"What if I have times when I just don't feel like being obedient?"

Let's go back to my husband's sage advice: Consider the source. Who is asking these questions? That's not your voice sowing seeds of doubt; it is Satan's voice. He wants to keep you in doubt and confusion. He wants you to pull off to the side of the intersection and remain ineffective. He wants you to fail to fulfill the purposes God has for you and thwart the positive impact you could make in the lives of so many.

You don't feel able? Good! Christ's power is made perfect through weakness (2 Corinthians 12:9). Ask God for the strength to persevere every day. Ask God for the desire to remain radically obedient and for spiritual eyes to see the radical blessings He will shower upon you.

What if you mess up? Grace! "God opposes the proud but gives grace to the humble. Submit yourselves, then, to God. Resist the devil, and he will flee from you. Come near to God and he will come near to you...humble yourselves before the Lord, and he will lift you up" (James 4:6-8,10). Please don't think I walk this radical obedience journey with perfection, because I don't. Chances are you won't either. But God doesn't expect perfection from us—He expects a person humble enough to admit her weaknesses and committed enough to press through and press on. He will guide us past the doubts and fears and lift us up to fulfill our calling.

What if you wake up in a bad mood and just don't feel like being obedient? Choice! Obey based on your decision to obey, not on your ever-changing feelings. *I don't feel like giving. I don't feel like smiling. I don't feel like listening to God.* But here's what God has to say about that: "It is *God* who works in you to will and to act according to his good purpose" (Philippians 2:13, emphasis added). When we ask God to continually give us the desire to remain obedient, He does. He will help us to want to obey Him and will give us His power to do so.

Get Ready!

If your answer is no to radical obedience, then let it be no. I just ask you to do one thing while you sit at the red light. Pray that God will give you the desire to say yes.

If your answer to this invitation is yes, then get ready. You have not only signed up for the most incredible journey you can imagine, but you've also just given God the green light to pour out His radical blessings on your life! What I'm writing about here is just a glimpse of how God will bless you. He's capable of so much more!

Deeper Relationship with God

You will begin to live in expectation of hearing from God every day. You will start to better understand His character and seek to be more like Him. You will discover the depth of love that the Father has for you that you never even knew possible. This will give you a feeling of acceptance and significance that you can't get any other way.

More Adventurous Life

I've heard it said that life would not be so hard if it weren't so daily. Yet the Bible says that each day is a gift from God that we should rejoice in (Psalm 118:24). Daily adventures with God will add an excitement to your life that will change your whole perspective. No longer is your day just one humdrum task after another but rather a string of divine appointments and hidden treasures waiting to be discovered.

Depth of Inner Peace

In our world of turmoil and uncertainty, there is nothing more precious than peace. When we say yes to God, we know that our life and the lives of those we love rest in the certainty of His never-changing love for us. While we can't control the circumstances we face, we can choose how we react to them. If you've settled in your heart to be radically obedient and to radically trust God, then you don't have to worry about the future. You will be blessed with the peace of knowing that God has a perfect plan and holds everything in His perfect control.

Personal Satisfaction

Radically obedient people no longer have to strategize and manipulate things into being. Instead, they are blessed with opportunities that bring them real satisfaction according to God's perfect design for them.

Better Relationships with People

In every relationship with others, you will find things that you love and things that, to be quite honest, get on your nerves. The radically obedient person is blessed with being able to appreciate another's Christlikeness and to give grace to their humanness. Whether a person is a believer or not, he is still made in God's image and God is crazy in love with him. When you are committed to radical obedience, you see everyone through God's eyes of love.

Meaning and Purpose to Life

Author Bruce Wilkinson wrote:

> Once the Lord has fed His child through intimate devotions, He begins to call him more pointedly to deeper obedience. At this point, the believer desires more of the Lord so much that he is more than willing to do whatever the Lord requires…Obedience for this individual is no longer a burden, undertaken only because the Bible tells him to do something. Rather, obedience becomes a joy because his closest friend and most compassionate Lord beckons him to be like Him.[1]

Our hearts search for deeper meaning in life, and radically obedient people find it in loving the Lord, loving others He brings in our path, and continually seeking to become more like Jesus.

Eternal Perspective

Life is about so much more than just the here and now, and the radically obedient person lives in light of that perspective. Life isn't about being comfortable and taking the easiest route; it's about living to give our lives away and making a real impact in this world. It's not about serving out of religious duty; it's about delighting in our relationship with God so much that we want to serve out of an overflow of love and gratitude. Our time here is but a small dot on an eternal line. What we do now in this brief moment will determine our destiny for eternity. The radically obedient person is blessed with an eternal perspective.

A Radically Obedient Example

I am drawn to the story of one New Testament woman who was radically obedient—Mary, Lazarus's sister. I am moved by Mary's overwhelming love for Jesus. She was a woman who understood the essence of radical obedience.

She knew when to listen and when to act. She knew when to simply sit at the Master's feet and when to pour out all she had in lavish love for her Lord (Matthew 26:6-13).

Jesus had just announced He would be crucified. Mary took what was probably her most costly possession, the perfume from her alabaster jar, and poured it out on Him. Normally, one would pour perfume on a dead body, but Mary anointed Jesus while He was still living. I believe it was so Jesus could carry the scent of her love with Him to the cross.

Mary was scolded by some of the disciples for her act of extravagance (naysayers!), but Jesus was quick to jump to her defense. What others saw as waste, Jesus saw as the purest form of walking out the gospel message. She was willing to love Him without reservation, without concern for what others might think or even concern for herself. Mary showed an unabashed love through this act, and, make no mistake, Jesus was quick to lavish His love right back on her. "I tell you the truth," Jesus said, "wherever the gospel is preached throughout the world, what she has done will also be told, in memory of her" (Matthew 26:13).

Isn't it amazing that such a small act of obedience could have such far-reaching effects? That can happen in our lives as well. Indeed, Mary was radically obedient and radically blessed…and you can be too.

How It Ends

Well, this whole adventure began with God telling me to give away my Bible, so is it any surprise that it ends the same way? Just last weekend I was flying to the Washington, DC, area for a speaking engagement. The man next to me on the plane was busy working on his computer and did not appear to be in the mood to be interrupted. My heart kept feeling drawn to share the gospel with him, but it didn't seem appropriate to force a conversation. So I prayed.

I prayed that God would prompt *him* to start talking to me. And talk he did. It wasn't long before he put his computer away and started asking me all kinds of questions about my career. Because I write and speak about Jesus, this was a perfect opportunity to tell him all about my Boss! When we started talking about God, he said he'd been studying the Koran and several other religious writings, but not the Bible. However, he'd called the friend he was traveling to see and asked if they could buy a Bible that weekend to complete his collection.

I almost fell out of my seat. Of all the planes traveling to Washington that day and of all the people who were seated together, God arranged for a man who needed a Bible to sit beside a woman who loves to give Bibles away! I shared with my new friend my passion for giving away

Bibles, and I promised I would send him one the next week. He sat stunned. When he finally spoke again, he told me he knew this was more than sheer coincidence. He knew God was reaching out to him.

Oh, my friend, we don't have to seek to create opportunities to live out our radical obedience. God has already gone before us and established them. We simply have to respond.

I pray that the end of this book is not the conclusion of your journey. I sincerely hope this is only the starting place, the point of inspiration and expression for you to live a radically obedient, radically blessed life.

SCRIPTURE FOR FURTHER STUDY ON RADICAL OBEDIENCE

God's Word has much to say on the topic of radical obedience and radical blessing. I encourage you to look up these key verses for yourself and discover what God wants you to know about His calling on your life.

Deuteronomy 28:1-14   Obedience opens God's storehouse of blessings.

2 Chronicles 16:9   God will strengthen the heart of the obedient person.

Esther 4:14   God has called you to obedience for such a time as this.

Psalm 15 Obedient people dwell in the presence and peace of God.

Psalm 24 Obedience in what you say, what you do, and what you think leads to holiness and blessings from God.

Isaiah 55:1-3 Obedience brings your soul satisfaction, delight, and new life.

Hosea 10:12 Obedience reaps the fruit of unfailing love and brings showers of righteousness.

Malachi 3:8-10 Being obedient givers will open God's storehouse of blessing.

Malachi 3:16-17 Radically obedient people are treasures to God.

Matthew 26:12-13 Even small acts of obedience have widespread effects.

Romans 1:5 Obedience comes from faith.

Romans 6:15-16	Obedience leads to righteousness.
Romans 8:5-6	Those walking in obedience have their minds set on God's desires.
2 Corinthians 9:6	The extent that we sow in obedience will determine the extent we will reap in blessings.
2 Corinthians 9:13	Men will praise God for the obedience that accompanies our faith.
Ephesians 4:24	We were created to be like God. We walk this out in obedience leading to holiness.
Philippians 2:13	It is God working in us that prompts us to be obedient and fulfill His good purpose.
Philippians 4:9	What you have learned, heard, or seen from God, walk it out in obedience and you will be blessed with peace.

2 Timothy 2:20-21 God is able to use the obedient person for His noblest purposes.

Hebrews 11 A list of radically obedient, radically blessed people.

1 Peter 1:13-14 Prepare your mind for obedience which leads to holiness.

1 Peter 2:21-22 Those who walk in obedience, walk in Jesus' footsteps.

1 John 2:3-6 Obedience makes God's love complete in us and enables us to walk as Jesus did.

NOTES

Chapter Two: Hearing God's Voice
1. *Life Application Study Bible (NIV)* (Wheaton, IL: Tyndale House Publishers, 1988), p. 2125.

2. Rick Warren, *The Purpose-Driven Life* (Grand Rapids, MI: Zondervan Publishing House, 2002), p. 233.

Chapter Three: When Obedience Becomes Radical
1. *Life Application Study Bible (NIV)* (Wheaton, IL: Tyndale House Publishers, 1988), p. 1632.

Chapter Four: You Never Know How God Will Use You Until You Let Him
1. *Life Application Study Bible (NIV)* (Wheaton, IL: Tyndale House Publishers, 1988), p. 2277.

Chapter Five: What Keeps Us from Radical Obedience

1. Rick Warren, *The Purpose-Driven Life* (Grand Rapids, MI: Zondervan Publishing House, 2002), p. 254.

2. Beth Moore, *Living Free* (Nashville, TN: LifeWay Press, 2001), p. 82.

3. Moore, *Living Free,* p. 77.

Chapter Six: If It Were Easy, It Wouldn't Be Worth Doing

1. Brent Curtis and John Eldredge, *The Sacred Romance* (Nashville, TN: Thomas Nelson, 1997), pp. 137-138.

Chapter Seven: Keeping Our Vision Clear

1. C.S. Lewis, *Mere Christianity* (San Francisco, CA: HarperCollins Publishers, 1952), pp. 149-50.

2. Max Lucado, *No Wonder They Call Him the Savior* (Sisters, OR: Multnomah Publishers, 1986), p. 126.

Chapter Eight: Giving Up What Was Never Ours

1. Randy Alcorn, *The Treasure Principle* (Sisters, OR: Multnomah Publishers, 2001), p. 57.

2. Elizabeth George, *A Woman's Walk with God* (Eugene, OR: Harvest House Publishers, 2000), p. 172.

Chapter Nine: Radically Blessed

1. Bruce Wilkinson, *Set Apart* (Sisters, OR: Multnomah Publishers, 1998) p. 175.

Lysa TerKeurst speaks nationwide
on this Radically Obedient, Radically
Blessed topic as well as others. To view
her schedule or to inquire about booking
her for your next conference or event,
log on to www.Proverbs31.org or call
Proverbs 31 Ministries toll free at
1-877-731-4663.

More Powerful Books
From Lysa TerKeurst

Capture the Heart of Your Spouse

These two practical paperbacks—one for wives and one for husbands—will open your eyes to the needs, desires and longings of your spouse. This great marriage-builder offers eight essential criteria plus creative tips for winning and holding his or her heart.
Available separately:
Capture His Heart
Capture Her Heart

Who Holds the Key to Your Heart?

In the hearts of most women lies a "secret place" containing hidden thoughts, painful experiences and emotions. Lysa TerKeurst, who has dealt with her own secret shame, will help you identify your pain and lead you to hope and healing through Scripture, testimonials, study questions and more. Paperback.

Leading Women to the Heart of God

Do you direct a women's ministry, lead a women's small group or hold a position somewhere in between? Even if you are simply considering a leadership role, start with this vital advice on developing a women's ministry. Learn the steps to start, build, expand and maintain your ministry for women. Paperback.

FOCUS ON THE FAMILY®
Welcome to the Family!

It began in 1977 with the vision of
Dr. James Dobson, a licensed psychologist
and author of best-selling books on marriage,
parenting, and family. Alarmed by the many pres-
sures threatening the American family,
he founded Focus on the Family, now an
international organization dedicated
to preserving family values through the
life-changing message of Jesus Christ.

• • •

For more information about the ministry,
or if we can be of help to your family, simply write to
Focus on the Family, Colorado
Springs, CO 80995 or call 1-800-A-FAMILY
(1-800-232-6459). Friends in Canada may write
Focus on the Family, P.O. Box 9800, Stn. Terminal,
Vancouver, B.C. V6B 4G3. or call 1-800-661-9800. Visit
our Web site at www.family.org
(in Canada, www.focusonthefamily.ca).

We'd love to hear from you!